Angela Porter's
DESIGNER DOODLES
HIDDEN PICTURES

Racehorse for Young Readers books may be purchased in bulk at special discounts for sales promotion, corporate gifts, fund-raising, or educational purposes. Special editions can also be created to specifications. For details, contact the Special Sales Department, Skyhorse Publishing, 307 West 36th Street, 11th Floor, New York, NY 10018 or info@skyhorsepublishing.com.

Racehorse for Young Readers™ is a pending trademark of Skyhorse Publishing, Inc.®, a Delaware corporation.

Visit our website at www.skyhorsepublishing.com.

10 9 8 7 6 5 4 3 2

Cover and interior artwork by Angela Porter

Print ISBN: 978-1-944686-55-0

Printed in China

Forever Inspired COLORING BOOK

Angela Porter's DESIGNER DOODLES
HIDDEN PICTURES

ANGELA PORTER

FOR YOUNG READERS

Find these hidden pictures throughout the following illustrations!

Designer Doodles

Ladybugs		93
Hearts		106
Cat heads		3
Stars		22
Candies		14
Buttons		46
Music notes		9
Raindrops		11

HIDDEN PICTURE
ANSWER KEY

1

2

3

4

5

6

7

8

9

10

11

12

13

14

15

16

17

18

19

20

21

22

23

24

25

26

27

28

29

30

31

32

33

34

35

PALETTE BARS

Use these bars to test your coloring medium and palette. Don't be afraid to try unique color combinations!